Mommy, I'm The Only one

Written by
Renee Scott Creese

Illustrated by
QBN Studios

Copyright © 2024 Renee Creese

All rights reserved.
No part of this book may be reproduced in any form or by any electronic or mechanical means, including information storage and retrieval systems, without written permission from the author, except for the use of brief quotations in a book review.

ISBN: 978-1-962725-00-2

Illustrated by QBN Studios

This book is dedicated to my parents, Basil and Perlina, whose sacrifice and devotion to their children and grandchildren is beyond what words can say. I love you both so much. The main character of this book, Lina, is named after Perlina, my mother.

I also thank my sister, Stacey and all of my friends and family whose love and support, gifts, texts, and phone calls meant the world to me during our daughter's medical challenges. I love you and I am grateful for each and everyone one of you.

I thank my wonderful husband Neigel, for his love, support and encouragement.

Lastly, I thank my beautiful daughters, Madison and Riley who inspired me to write this book. I am so incredibly proud of you both and I am so honored to be your Mom.

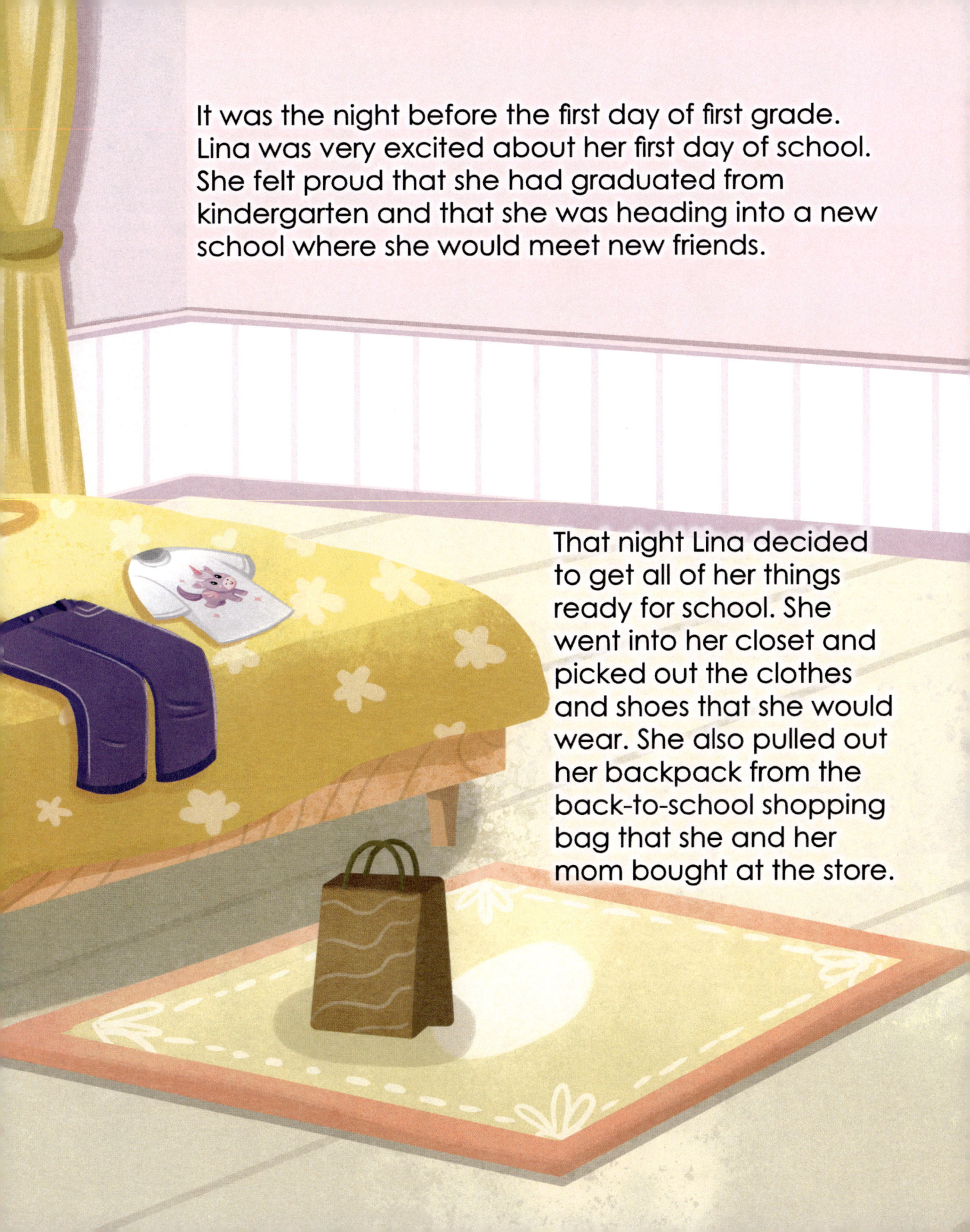

It was the night before the first day of first grade. Lina was very excited about her first day of school. She felt proud that she had graduated from kindergarten and that she was heading into a new school where she would meet new friends.

That night Lina decided to get all of her things ready for school. She went into her closet and picked out the clothes and shoes that she would wear. She also pulled out her backpack from the back-to-school shopping bag that she and her mom bought at the store.

Lina pulled out her lunch box and asked her mom if she could pack her snacks for school the next day. Lina's mother smiled and said "I know you are excited about tomorrow, but you must get some sleep! We have to get up early so that you can ride the bus!"

Lina was excited about riding the bus just like her big sister, Kaley!

Everything about first grade was so exciting. She couldn't wait to show off her new backpack, her lunchbox, her glitter unicorn shirt and her tennis shoes that lights up when she jumps!

"Ok Lina, it's time for bed! We want to have an early start tomorrow," prodded her mom. So Lina went to bed filled with excitement!

The next morning, Lina's mother went into her room to wake her up. To her mother's surprise, Lina was already in the bathroom brushing her teeth! Her mother smiled, and said "Wow, aren't you the early bird!"

"Mommy I gotta get ready. I don't want to miss the bus!" replied Lina anxiously.

"Ok Lina, I made your favorite blueberry pancakes." Lina's eyes lit up! She got dressed and ran to the kitchen to eat Mom's yummy pancakes.

Beep beep! She could hear the school bus coming down the hill. "Mommy, the bus is here!"

She screamed with excitement as she raced through the front door. The bus came to a stop.

The doors opened and Lina climbed in feeling like a big girl.

"You must be Lina", the bus driver said.

"Yes and I'm going to be in first grade!"

She took her seat next to the window so she could wave to her mother. The bus made one more stop and then arrived at her new school.

Everything seemed so much bigger than preschool. When Lina arrived to her classroom, she saw her teacher and all the smiling faces of her classmates. Her day was filled with activities.

She read books,  did some math,

writing,  art,

she had lunch  and of course recess.

When Lina went out for recess, Lina heard some children laughing, so she went over to play with them. They looked at her and started laughing.

"Your hair is like cotton candy, giggled Milly". When Lina looked around, she didn't see anyone else with hair like hers. She didn't see anyone else that looked like her at all. She realized that she was the only black girl in her class.

Lina began to feel a little lonely. When the bell rang for everyone to go back to class, she wasn't as excited. She could still hear some of the children laughing at her. She was sad. On the ride home after dismissal, Lina looked around on the school bus and no one else looked like her on the bus either. She hadn't realized that in the morning.

When the bus came to her bus stop, Lina saw her mom waiting at the bus stop. Lina's mother was all smiles.

"Hi Lina, how was your first day of school?!" Her mom asked excitedly.

Lina looked very different from when she left the house in the morning. Lina's mother realized that there was no smile on her face.

"What's wrong sweetheart? Didn't you have a fun first day of school?" Her mother asked.

"It started off fun, but then it ended not so fun. I don't want to go back to school!"

"Why? What happened?" Her mother asked.

"The kids all laughed at me. Mommy, I'm the only one with fluffy hair. I'm the only one that's black. I'm the only one!!!!" Cried Lina. "I don't want to have fluffy hair anymore. Everyone was pointing and laughing!"

"Ohhhhh, I see," said Lina's mother. "Come here, my love." Lina's mother gave her a big hug and wiped away her tears.

"Well do you know that everyone has something special and different about themselves?" asked Lina's mom.

"Some people have fluffy hair. Some have curly hair, lighter skin, darker skin, freckles, and I could go on and on. But there are so many things that make us all special and unique in our own way," Mom continued.

"The kids in your class probably have never seen fluffy hair before. And yes, you probably are the only one with fluffy hair and that's ok. Many times when we see something different or new, some people might laugh or even stare. But Lina, I want you to know that you are beautifully and wonderfully created by God. God loves your fluffy hair and so do I," said mom encouragingly.

So, when you go to school tomorrow, remind your friends that your hair is one of the many things that makes you unique and special. We are all different and our differences make us special. You are beautiful and don't you ever forget that. Don't let anyone make you feel bad about who you are, ok Lina?"

When they got inside the house mom asked Lina, "Want to see something?" Lina's mom took her own hair out of her braided ponytail and she showed Lina her natural long and fluffy hair!

Lina said "Wowwww, Mom you never take your hair down and I have never seen your hair down before! It's so beautiful!!!"

"Thank you my love, and as you can see Mommy's hair is also naturally fluffy."

Lina's mom pulled out some old pictures and she showed Lina some pictures of the many different styles she has worn her hair in over the years.

"See, I can wear it in a ponytail , I can wear it in braids, I can put beads on the braids, I can wear it in cornrows, I can wear it naturally curly (or fluffy as you call it) and I can even wear it straight if I want. So you see, there are lots of different ways to wear your hair and that also makes you special!"

So, the next day when Lina went to school she noticed some of the kids staring at her. But she remembered what her mommy said to her. She decided to tell the kids exactly what her Mom told her.

"God made me beautiful and God made my beautiful fluffy hair. We are all different and beautiful." The kids in Lina's class smiled.
Milly said "Lina I like your hair. It's so cool!! I'm sorry I laughed at your hair yesterday."

"That's ok. Let's promise to be kind!" Lina said.

"Wanna play, Lina?" And in an instant, all of the kids who were laughing at her the day before, wanted to play with her today. She had the best day ever!

So if you ever find yourself being the only one, no matter where you are, just remember that God loves all of us and he made us all special. You are unique and beautiful with many special gifts to share with the world. Don't let anyone make you feel bad about your differences. You are amazing!

THE END

Made in the USA
Middletown, DE
18 September 2024